MW01622633

Jokes by

HENLEY BELLE JOHNSON

Edited by

ELLE MULIARCHYK JOHNSON

Illustrated by

ANNA DALBUZ

For many more jokes, videos and fun
go to
https://www.jokesbykids.fun/

Meet us on Instagram!
@ellemuliarchyk
@bluebini

Printed and bound in Canada
ISBN 978-0-692-12425-3 (Hardcover)

For DADDY BUDDY

Dear Readers,

Henley and I invite you to get imaginative
and playful, absurd and silly together.
There are no wrong answers!
We hope this will inspire you to come up
with jokes of your own.

Let this book fill you with the joy of a childhood spirit,
and with all of the love that we have put into it.

ELLE & HENLEY

What's a horse's favorite drink?

LEMO-NEIGH-D!!

What underwear does a Zebra wear?

A Z-BRA !!

What's a cow's favorite bird?

E-MOO!!

What does grass say to the gardener who waters it?

GRASS-iAS!!

What's a Brachiosaurus' favorite vegetable?

BRACH-OLI!!

What does a Dilophosaurus do before going to bed?

FLOSS!!

What does a Velociraptor put on his pancakes?

CiR-RUP!!

What type of candy did
archaeologists find in the Pyramids?

PYRAMINTS

PYRA-MINTS!!

How does a slug feel in the morning before his cup of coffee?

SLUG-GISH!!

What personality does a vitamin have?

VITA-MEAN!!

What do toes
eat for breakfast?

TOE-ST!!

And what do LEGS eat?
-Eggs!

AND THIS IS NOT A JOKE!

A hundred years ago cars were seen as an environmentally friendly solution to HORSES. Before cars, there were 200,000 horses living in New York City and every horse pooped 30 pounds of poop everyday. Get out your calculators. That's 6 million pounds of poop. Every single day.

LEMONS are full of vitamin C that can prevent the disease scurvy. This desease was common among sailors stuck on ships for months. Even today, the British Navy requires ships to carry enough lemons so that every sailor can have one ounce of juice a day.

The stripes on ZEBRAS aren't just for show. They help to protect them from predators. In the wild, when lions, who are colorblind, see a herd of zebras, all those stripes bunched together look like a field of tall grass.

A COW drinks a bathtub of water a day, They have an excellent sense of smell and can detect odors up to six miles away.

It takes 8 weeks for EMU eggs to hatch, and it's the Dad who sits on them until they do. During that time, he does not eat. His body uses its stored fat for energy. The dad also raises the chicks for the next 18 months, taking them to feeding places and teaching them what to eat.

Bamboo is not a tree. It's a type of GRASS that grows 120 feet high!
A 50x50 foot Grass lawn produces enough oxygen to sustain a family of four.

BRACHIOSAURUS had a lifespan of 100 years. Scientists used to think that they spent a lot of time in the water and used their long necks as a periscope, some people believe that the Loch Ness Monster is really a 150-million-year-old Brachiosaurus.

If all the dental FLOSS sold in the USA in a single year were place end to end, it would stretch 3 million milies. Thats a trip to the Moon and back SIX times! It removes the plaque that hosts 300 different types of harmful bacteria. Dental floss is often used to break out of prison: in Wisconsin prisoners braided floss into a 18-foot rope and escaped over the prison walls.

Maple SYRUP is full of magnesium and 65 different antioxidants. A few spoons on your pancakes delivers as many antioxidants as a cup of broccoli or tomato.

Sharks have a lot of teeth, but a SLUG has even more – 27,000 teeth!

COFFEE is the second most traded commodity on earth after oil. There are 25 million farmers in over 50 countries involved in producing coffee.

Your FEET have 26 bones – that's one quarter of all the bones in your entire body.